Josephine in the Mirror

Poems of Life Told From a Women's Eyes

By Sophia Richards Whitter, BA, MBA.

Copyright © Sophia Richards

All rights reserved. No part of this book may be reproduced in any form or by any electronic or mechanical means, including information storage and retrieval systems, without permission in writing from the publisher, except by reviewers, who may quote brief passages in a review.

"Every great dream begins with a dreamer. Always remember, you have within you the strength, the patience, and the passion to reach for the stars to change the world."
-Harriet Tubman

*Whenever A People
or An Institution
Forgets its Hard Beginnings
It is Beginning to Decay.
- Carl Sandburg 1963*

Dedication

This book is dedicated to women who have bridged the chauvinist quota that was set out to place them in life. Women who have chosen to chart their own path to success in life, who chose roles that society said were for men and are unwoman-like.

Firstly, I dedicate this book to my mother, Avis Nenita Henry. She is my first encounter with a strong woman and the strongest woman in my records. A single parent mother who taught me always to find a way through the dark times and that faith paired with hard work transcends sweet success.

As this book looks at the strength of women to overcome obstacles and strive for greatness, even exerting themselves in roles traditionally deemed masculine, nonetheless, women of today's time and some in history are brought to the mind and are mentioned in some of the poems within. The dedication is extended to:
1. Nanny of the Maroons[1]: The Ashanti[2] warrior who fought against British enslavement. Through guerilla tactics and brevity, she freed enslaved Africans. She established the first free village in Jamaica and stands today as the country's only national heroine.

---

[1] Maroons - Ashanti Africans who settled in Jamaica and established the first free village in the Blue Mountains on the Eastern side of the Island.
[2] Ashanti - African tribe in West Africa.

2. The Hon Portia Simpson Miller: The first female prime minister to be appointed in Jamaica. The baton was given to her by her predecessor, The Hon P.J. Patterson, then later she ran for the position and won the seat of Prime Minister against her opposition. She showed me that women can attain the highest governmental public office in Jamaica.
3. Michelle Obama: The first lady who, with grace and determination, showed me that a strong sense of self is all a woman needs to be fierce on the world stage of life.
4. Congresswoman Alexandria Ocasio - Cortez: The Congresswoman who displayed immense composure in the face of chauvinism. With confidence, she exposed her humble beginnings, which encouraged a woman like myself to pursue her American Dream in equity.
5. Hillary Clinton: The first woman to be nominated on America's major political platform. Her journey to the nominations taught me that a woman can go as far as she sees herself and even beyond the success she has not yet imagined or dreamt of.

Acknowledgment

Any attempt to create provoke thoughts on the beginning of life. I hereby thank God for the strength to remain on this creative journey despite the challenges of temporary homelessness, depression, and financial struggles. Faith sheltered me, elevated me, and paid me through kinds.

Many thanks to my aunt, Dr. Yvette Molajo, who continues to be a source of strength for me. She is a symbol of academic accomplishment and a strong believer in my work. Her frequent phone calls, checking on the newest happenings in my life, my newest projects, etc., consistently motivate me to take on new challenges.

I would like to thank Andrew Dixon, a true friend whose support goes beyond encouragement. Late night conversations on emerging topics in politics, or life in general, inspired me and kept me alert through the most difficult times of my life.

My undying gratitude to the following people who reviewed this book: Miss Shonelle Price, Mr. Alston Hemmings, Miss Yolande Harris, and Miss Mirla Gudiel. Your respective areas of expertise, background in the performing art, English Literature, academia, and creative art are the tools that helped to refine the work within.

Much appreciation to Attorney Jessica Mayo. She taught me that brevity to present my truth will be all the defense I need in life. Your advice gave me strength to stand in the face of adversaries and in this work, I bear my truths as a badge of honor rather than unhappiness and shame.

Thanks to my exceptional Publisher, Sierra Dean, for being patient with me and believing in my vision for this book and extended gratitude to an Ogoni of my ancestral land.

……….. Thanks to all guiding forces from the Mother Land.

Table of Contents

Dedication i
Acknowledgements iii

◊◊◊

Section I 1
    Memories From the Nothingness 2
    Covered Youth on Loopy Path 3
    Diamond in the Rocks 4
    Revealed in a Dream 5
    The Other in a Woman 6
    Arm An Geddon 8
    Sickness in the Veins 9
    Ghetto Candy Man-Remembering Compton St. 10
    Rally for Feminine Diplomacy "Hillary Clinton"-2016 12
    In Memory of Dear Al 14
    Life Source Contaminant 15
    Gin-Her Daddy's Drink 17
    Leather Soul 18
    Sound Of Freedom 21
    Forbidden Or Not It's Love 24
    Acknowledging My Mother Who Died to Live Again 26
    The Story 27
    Freezing Cold 29
    A Lover's Wishful Eyes Watching the Tears of a Familiar Sky 32

Slave of a Kind 35

Mi Bandana 36

From the Lawns 38

New York Times 40

Bosom Of My Love 42

◊◊◊

John Tom's Love Letter 44

◊◊◊

Hillary In Line 47

Knitting Hands 48

Hollywood's Poortraits 49

To The Heaven from Sorrow 51

The Colors in Me to The World Out There 52

Black Seeds of Ferguson St. Louis 2014 54

A Man's Wife and Life to Take 56

Heart Of the Brain 58

An Arousal of The Long Forgotten 59

◊◊◊

Voices from the Ocean's Floor for Ben Solomon Carson 61

Street Talk of Immigrants in Glee 62

The Move 64

For Josephine 65

Tender Flesh 66

Simple Life 67

Home Away from Home 68

On The Day Of Pentecost 70

Grandpa's Radio 71

Imagine If I Tried 72
The Joy I Bled.. 73
The Yellow Tail That Never Sings 75

◊◊◊

For The Brevity of Sowore; Brother From My Mothers Land 77
Body Politics 79
Gberemene George Floyd of my Father's Land 81
Minnesota Protests 83
Africans in Motion: From Plantations to Boulevards........ 84
Grey Thoughts in the Black Abyss 85

◊◊◊

Section II.. 87
The Colonizers – Abatement of Xamaca 88
To My Country's Queen Elizabeth II............................... 90
For When the Son of Men Shall Stand 92
Highness Mama Tell Jesse Mi Coming Home 93
Wig Wearing Magistrates-Pass The Crown..................... 95

◊◊◊

Annie B: A Life Severed Too Soon 98
The Deaf Tone Of Politics 100
The Fight of The Cousins; White Power. 102
Black Girl: Corporate Commodity Of Commerce 104

◊◊◊

Caravans Of Ukranian Refugees: They Call Them By Their Nationality; Ukranians 108
The Day 400 Plus Wrote Their Names in The Streets 111
Royalty at Rest- 09/19/2022 112

Epilogue	114
Letter to the Oppressor and the Human Resource	115
Glossary	121
About the Author	127

Section I

The Life of an Island Girl is quite simple yet complex in the plethora of experiences it offers. Living in Jamaica in the small District of Cotton Piece makes my life less of an adventure to many. However, it is the life of neighbors, friends and family members that adds richness to the meaning of life for me. As Josephine I provoke the consciousness of Christians evoking the essence of Joseph the Dreamer, yet chaotic, experiencing life boundlessly venturing into historical periods that are virtually impossible for my physical presence. The many journeys of the variety of characters mark the transformation of a single major character. Bearing multiplicity of characterization spanning several names, age groups, lifestyles, cultures, geographic locations across time zones, my collective selves are relatable to the common man.

Memories From the Nothingness

If only tomorrow was so clear
Today wouldn't be dark blue and gray overall
But in theory it's meant to be
Preserving the surprise mode; the soul to life
Day breaks and cherished sunsets
Flower blooms and dreary Winters
From green leaves to rusty stems
In the borrows and meadows life seems a mystic
Yet timed as each move is anticipated; sequenced
To show beauty in ripples
But when man cease to be,
Beaten in the collapse of time,
Cocooned for earth's nourishment
There's never been more surprised faces,
Untamed wailing and black and white parading
Where's the surprise for his sordid fate?
Since this too is meant to be-
I'll water not my pillows
I'll think of the memories in glee
Drink in the pleasures of my seasonal Lilies
Attend to my delicate Orchids
And ran about on Cotton flurries treading on gentle winds
Swirling and rolling between Dandelions grown in grass
So green;
It seems like a piece of Davinci's Dream.

Covered Youth on Loopy Path

Tiptoeing to a Jinga Janga[3] Tune
Bobbing and weaving; looking lopsided
Rocking smoking and nodding

Mauled by voices of the dim
Strange loathing figures afar
Cedar cabinets and panel shutters
Rust ridden swing spreading and sighing faintly
Spiraled in-
Smaller and smaller my corner grew,
Brown Leather waved about
Ripping my flesh without doubt
Sending my screams to the world out

But metal shutters matched the effort fought
Sweat and rivery tears carved me on wooden floors
Red channeled back and front my cotton dress-
Cherry Juice spills today I attest

Fragments of an image most grotesque
And never had I more regrets.

---

[3] Jinga Janga - Crazy up and down tune.

Diamond in the Rocks

I need this Winter at bay
And berry Sumer to stay
Madness and hunger to remain gray
Noondays and tender kisses for early May
Rain Clouds and soft earth to sway

Glistening streams all solid molds
Church bell chilled and grossly tolls
No pigeons prancing lazy wings
No flowers racing time's dongs and dings
Sad faces dangling on drooped shoulders
While drunkards share with women of no owners

Foreign, all in this land I see
And in the rocks I hold to me.

Revealed in a Dream

Barking dogs in Scarlet light
Pensiveness a crave for thou
Daynight scene I called it too
Never a more lushful backdrop
A world for all and only one can see
For weathered days mildew the spree
And muck thrash the canvas
Mixing colors of odds
In the stillness an attempt at art
I'll lend a match to raise the ash
A thought before I crash
For a king size is only resting shed
But for two;
It's more than a bed
Counting sheep in a lofty green
Shutting the windows for the deep
And returning with nothing for keeps
And when my doll chimes
I'll reach that place of old times
Laden with white and natural pines
Blue lights and silver lines
His pale skin gleam like of figurines
Daybreaks and pierce
Through my panes.

The Other in a Woman

No!!!! She shouted
Strong mournful yellings,
She's distressed for her tenderling;
A mere thought, hungry for somewhere to belong
Blood bubbling and legs shaking
Terror quickened the place I held her dearest
And each beat battered my ribs, puncturing my walls,
Heaven turned its back,
Hell's fury is never ending;
An earthquake unleveled my grip on reality,
Searching for my savior I tilted my head
With drenched cheeks
Looking for a kiss of Sunshine
Instead, the host of heaven spat in the scorned face
Covered with the shame from neglecting its maker
My head swung to the dust
Sending hope to No Man's Land.
Swishing crazily,
Half mashed and bleeding a worm traveled toward a rock
Flat on my belly I crawled,
Slowly among shit and old refuse
Watching the careless queer creature-
It stopped frozen wet with water from above
Countless minutes passed then it reawakened
Moving rapidly looking all white and whole
Not noticing the cry of the black-eyed crow
It courses its map to the Rock

Made whole by the long awaiting washing,

Seems it fueled its journey;
A mere thought seeing the flimsy creature had
somewhere he belonged.
Rising to a full stance
Eyes beaming a new radiance
The rain cleaned the mirrors of my Harley
I flung myself on the cold leathered seat
Ready to forget old lies and unwarranted deceit.

Arm An Geddon[4]

For a soul does magnify this sole
For a heart does mourn the earth
For the God in him we kneel
For the heavens beyond me all men craves
And from the hell in me I retreat

When rivers made blood shows fishes carcasses,
The fields lay bare with plagued grains
Ice rocks pelted from above
And skins break free with legion purging the man of the rocks
I stand resolute with a salute for the Kingdom of Heaven.
History rides on the back of legends
Time spins its hands rhythmical to myths
And by these stories;
People smiles, fears and tears all
Are prompted
and halted.

---

[4] Arm an Geddon - Play on the word Armageddon.

Sickness in the Veins

In Hunger games for my soul
I watched the two
I stand aloof the leopards of the Valley
Feeling neither regret nor vengeance
Spying through the window of my world
Dark elements strapped the boots of life
Under the coat of fear
As the fear clung the organs
The Upper Drummer beat a Gothic thumb
While my veins scrunched to the stink of the blood
A bitter gall hunt for sweetness
For the grim reapers, insurgency is the worst emergency.
Hours passed upside-down heads
Wide mouths, starched grins
Sprawled legs estranged from dangling hands
Free
But yoked to a half-made corpse
Fit to be lumbered on the chariot for hell's furnace
Yet the door to the right is left ajar
Maybe his hurry to a chosen soul left it so
I dared not to enter
By Mercy he might give me right to rent a center.

Ghetto Candy Man-Remembering Compton[5] St.

Candy, here comes the Candy man
He's the back yard Daddy
Dishing sweets for the sour
Stealing kids dream a million
I saw him one day
Riding his ghetto dragon
Dashing the monster hard down Compton
It's not at the sight of red or blue lights coming down his way
But the one who stopped to play
His steely teeth dazzled the sun
Clouds rushed to shun it numb
The damage is already done
And the bloody moon waltzed the night's tune
Like Deja Vu morn had another to pay
Candy, here comes the Candy man
Circling the harbor far away
Tadpoles swirling in puddles;
Huddled in the shadows of the gangway[6]
Breaking today's dark to sell bitter sweets.

Distributed only by young mobile stores;
The tenderling of the poors

---
[5] Compton - Street that crosses the street Keokuk on South Grand Avenue in St Louis Missouri.
[6] Gangway - Urban language in America means narrow walkways between buildings, almost like an alley.

Such sweets aren't listed mono or disaccharides:
Crystals that hyper your mind
Concoctions making you hysterically inclined…….
………….. twinkle twinkle little star
………….. how I wonder what you are.

Rally for Feminine Diplomacy "Hillary Clinton"-2016

Woman of the hills
A heroine we see
A queen born to be free
But when men dealt the cards of chains
Another mother and maker she's deemed
If her curtain's not lifted the nation's number would not be,
Still her worth's trivialize
Can't she be glorified among hunters and conquerors of our times?
One voice and common views, she sees with the eyes like yours.
Who said the pants make the business deal more sealed?
Or does it merely coax the ego of boars?

If only they could see the strength of the heroine on the Island rock
Traveling to countries far and wide
Sealed the deals firm gripped and wave welcome first world Aristocrats
Private jetters and famous society gallivanters, she kissed them all

Whether skirt or pants
Black or white a woman has no place among these dominants,
Still she solicits numbers to secure her place

Marking another moment of man's ego to support conventions

Dare not call it chauvinism for that too is old
Cheers to her debating with fire under the blue skies
And may the whiteness of her words defeat trumping lies

A heroine we see
A queen born to be free.

In Memory of Dear Al

Cursing and weeping Debbie hugged her third male that she dearly loves
For this was all that had left of her sugar plum
Taken away early by the contradicting arms of death;
Indeed, death was far, he looked as free and contented as a proud puss
But what thunders over the north can only cause tremors at the South
After the shocked hearts went cracking, and even big brains started busting trying to figure.
Was it planned by him who's in every storm or the wretched Lord of hell?
Begotten in abundant love he was. So why put such dark and deadly metal to your head?
Such a wonder for a dove and a radiant sunshine he was in people's lives
Tormented, his mind and physical being battling the harshness of gambling
Like Samson rigorously ripping the beast jaws
Uncle separated a man such as Adrian[7] from his finances and yet he
No matter what they tried, to keep him from the Casino paws
He always found a way and to this problem there weren't any existing laws.

---

[7] Adrian - My cousin who shot himself.

Life Source Contaminant

Between Rose breasts are the roots and the bed for thorns
If one believes its lie, then all the cocks can testify
For they have crowed several mornings and nights
Deserting humble housewives for what they value in "high esteems"
Carrying frankincense, myrrh and often gold for the sole they praise
And these are all good for an upset stomach is restored and debts are settled,
But gratitude must be extended for the master builder's work of awe
Just enough to send welcome running to her as if its feet were all ignited.

Sure the repercussions are dry and long lasting
Lots of them travel around and bashful blames are casting
From the Northern to the Southern Coast of the water-land
She caused very dark and light skinned bodies to be hopelessly purging through hives
And even Aristocrats to be laid to rest in houses with heads too low to the ground to be seen
Continuously she dangles dangerously in the sight of men who have roamed for her nude show.

"……….the feminization of Joseph the Dreamer of the Old Testament is observed as a direct feminist approach to telling the simple experiences of the life I have lived and the life I still dream of, standing as Josephine in the Mirror. These simple experiences such as birthing, death, marriage, and laughter are the experiences that make life meaningful for humans and in turn determine the quality of life we live overall. At times you will see me living fewer desirable lifestyles. I am taken by circumstances of poverty, bitterness, and mangled by the treacherous ways of the streets. As my confidant you will see that depression and alcoholism are merely challenges and as such allow the everyday man to relate to said imperfections."

Gin-Her Daddy's Drink

If love blunders, why is it the biggest score?
And if it never ends how come two became torn?
Like weed straddled roses they struggled bruising their heels
They dashed[8] across deserts and plains
Dragging decades of dust and rust
Residues from places familiar and beyond the unknown
Finding comfort on the strangest paths
Trading along the danger zones
And if the journey isn't already hard, try the vices that forced the mind
Along the tavern walls a back is rested as one turn to the ills of the night
Morning break and the gut release its stinks
The hangover set the drag for this day
The stench of liquor caresses her dress
The fringes along her hem soaked in the gutters gunk
Slurred words struggled from her mouth
Piss fragranced clothes and mascara smudged face
Toppling and leaning this figure
Hers the remains of the night's wilds.

---

[8] Dashed - To be put aside or abandoned.

Leather Soul

Straight, thick black hair
A prominent eye-wart sensing an approach from a distance,
A broad waist and a corn sticking from each big toe;
Telling all when the rain is going to fall
By an unbearable swelling pain that impeded motions of the feet
Were the markers of a woman I loved.

I learn the colors of the Rainbow from her coat of many colors
Kept just for teaching me that my world is more than Black and White;
Teaching me that all that's on the surface is mere White hiding the blackness of generations of lies and guilt.........
Many called her Indian and worst of them all coolie[9].
Her pinched lips held back the tongue that would freely swear and cursed the name givers;
Once there weren't any strangers around.

Called her Maroon and fulfilling her high expectation
Those same lips would have curled into a cunning ninety eight year old smile,
revealing not only a harmless mouth
But a side of the old skeleton that resisted death and fought for life beyond this generation;

---

[9] Coolie - Jamaican word for a person of African and Indian mixed descent. Once used to label a person as half breed.

A life that was traveling but was stubborn to take a rest
The type of rest that ensured all activities were ceased;
Locking down engine work making the Human shell
To be nothing but a chosen shell to house the spirit that live to be free;
Not bounded by love or any strong emotions such as hate
But cleverly commanded in a whisper through mere air
To keep itself steady in a particular shell until it's given further orders.

It is no man's wish to end their time
Sleeping, feasting and idly passing each hour ignoring details of everyday life;
Details about each life that was and is at that moment;
They refuse to treasure the slightest movement of a branch or the dips and slides left by a hurricane................
Instead we live to harm the shell
Directly or indirectly-
Always in favor of the pockets
Developing or demolishing in the quest for life?
Although sounding ironical
This is man's fate and his biggest accomplishment;
Making and destroying
Surely it's never intentional when he becomes the target of his own aim.
Blessed are her days
Nothing missed her half blinded eyes
Teaching, observing all and lived
Making the most of nothing

Saving from everything, leaving specific colors in this world
Not oil or water paint for walls and boards-
The type of colors that she wished her days were to be painted with.

All three sisters of time watched her intently
Noting her to be a specimen from a broken mold
The first measured ninety-eight years' worth of beautiful stripes
As one read it contemplating an extension
The other impatiently chopped the tape, releasing the spirit prematurely
Forcing Great Gran Ernestine Garvey to the black box.
The type of upcoming event that not even the wart could forewarned against;
The entire body was dead to the call of times.....................

Sound Of Freedom

And when the Abeng[10] bellowed the Animal Cry
He shivered with white fear as if he had seen a ghost
While the 'others' jumped and danced the freedom jig
Laughing, chanting and summoning the dancers of yesterday; carefully teaching those of tomorrow.
Not holding back any sorrow
The smiles hurriedly converted into rivers of tears
Mapping the path to the promise land
Revealing the water troubled by God;
Troubled for it has washed several feet
Setting thee galloping like the hunter's horses
Or like the blood thirsty hounds that were rewarded for their black deeds.

And when the Abeng bellowed the animal cry
The feet that were taken; making examples of the disobedient
Stumped the impatient dance of freedom,
The detached hands that were stolen
Clapped the tune that propelled the dance for freedom
And drummed the madness of the moment into the violated women belly,
Inspired the willow looking contortion of the old
Whose backs were overworked into their crooked form
While the completely silenced
And permanently paralyzed surfaced

---

[10] Abeng - The Cow horn blown by Africans. They used to signal each other and for warnings.

Through possessions of the freedom dancers
Announcing their happiness of the historical dance,
Empowering any weakness sensed in a dancer's spirit.

And when the Abeng bellowed the animal cry
White fear increased for it calls a warning threatening Babylon[11]
And hoarding distress into the bosom of the vile and heartless.
Owls howled and dogs hooted
Parents knew the White lies
The children eyes were opened
Reading the tales of the future in blood on the great walls
Like an oracle the wall disclosed the future;
Fires of nights and dark days
Parallel to cold wars and world wars
Leaving houses in ruins
And threatening the wealthy's supply-
The table turned with the servers being white with terror and the sitters;
Twitched in their tethered and stained, black garments.

And when the Abeng bellowed the animal cry
All but the Master knew-
Disciplined bodies would be free,
His mansion will be red hot from the outskirts of the clearing,
White fear would meet Black anger;
Face to face in combat for the 'self',

---

[11] Babylon - Jamaican reference for Government and its affiliates.

Refusing the persona of the 'other'
On the grounds of the need for Life
At the pour when the Abeng bellowed the Animal Cry.

Forbidden Or Not It's Love

Open your eyes and behold-
Let your fortunes before-told
From whence I came is an unbreakable mold
Why not!! Enjoy your gift of a body
Too strong to be handled weak
Too compassionate to be speared of love

Be: that special breath of wind blowing my hair back
The daring rush that cause my blood to course restlessly
The fire which kindles continuously within me' the lion desire to hunger
No!! Not that of food but to be yearning for the touch;
Triggering goose pimples and tightening my stride on the mountain of life.

I wonder is that too much to ask for?
Comparing Blackness to Redness in that light of retreat
I would agree a succulent berry she is indeed
Only fair then her needs are to be pleased
Hey!!! Yes you, are you man enough to feed????

Like death you stare me in the eye
With vibrating hands and a firm flawless salute down below
Why then not devour my flesh creating bruises of love
In places so far and delicate only YOU can touch?

Reality rocked upon me like an angry storm

And awakening from my comma form
I acknowledge the blatancy of the world.
Yes we are playing a game of the heart
That's the time when only day and night tells
us APART......................................

Acknowledging My Mother Who Died to Live Again

Charred by memories wild
Mother slept on a thorn's head
Tormented like a trapped Soul
She turned restlessly
But, for a second the sheet a new revealed
Teeth exposed by the retreating lips.
I wondered was she finally happy?
Had she at last found merriment?
This I must ask.
For all knew that day she wore a mask
Too early!!!!!! I beckoned.
Disillusionment rocked her heart
As slowly from this world she hastily departed
Oh! Open your eyes, isn't life sweet;
Forsake not your chicks
Who at your feet looks on in glee
Faith chased away the gray clouds
And once more to Morning Miste and Starshine
Her windows opened.......

The Story

Oh yes! Moving from pig slums to Castles of her heart,
Working from her thighs to her chest,
Covering West Kingston to the North Coast
Showing no prejudice, she searched for herself
In her search owing no one
Depending strongly on instincts and blessings.
This girl told herself that there were cosmic forces shielding her health
And opening doors;
Literally opening her doors
No! This is nothing new
It is similar to Samson and Delilah
Making sure they fall with blinding heaviness
Like Adam and Eve coercing the flesh to give in
Leaving them empty and with festering
Stinking wounds in a Job like patience
Wounds that would take a miracle to be cured.
Yes this is Ghetto grandmothers' story, sisters and Aunties,
Traversing the long road of success
Without a definite trade at the moment
Having no plantation inheritance from blood thirsty patrons who claimed from innocent Blackness.

Only a trail of the worth she once possessed.
Affordable caresses, clawing out their wages.

Weeping from tired feet and a story of penetrating harshness
Screaming in ecstatic sadness
Envisioning the Degree
Fulfilling the dream of a castle,
Outstretched lawn, car
and only One Man
With playful children guarded by canine power.

Dying slowly the dream vanishes
And closed hands released their grip,
Collecting perspiration and other body wetness as his length declined.

Candy held tight to her body
Like a map her body revealed the path;
Of masculine touches from the moments of conquests-
Yesterday to now and when it all began;
The Day of her fourteenth Birthday.

Freezing Cold
The helpless daughter bear's witness

Staring at the bedside not looking directly in his eyes-
I wonder how alive are his thoughts?
Ignoring the clattering sounds of limb against the pane I tried to make music:
The type he loved
Pressing my lips against the harmonica and stomping my feet
Harming the hard floor with each blow;
But still he remains quiet and motionless.
I thought how beautiful is death and how calm does he look?

Two days before he called on his only daughter:
Doctor insisted thorough rest and deep massage,
Take medication on the clock,
Ignore all meats and my favorite pork hock.
Sounds like serious business

What?

He can't have anything fatty demands of Mr. Doc.

I agree with every word and that's the reason why;
I left out sugar and salt
From your porridge substituting tin milk with Cow's milk
Grandma serenaded the house with prayers

Casting out demons and avoiding pagans:
God of Abraham, Joshua and Moses......
Cautiously administering spiritual, Formal and Informal dosages
Hoping to stop his skin lesions.

Exchanging meat for meat he bargained with the maid
Stealing through the dark kitchen like a rat
She handed over the rich and dark fatty flesh He devilishly rubbed his hands together
With love for both meats
One is dead and the other alive waiting to be carved by him.

Betrayed by the everyday ritual of his cock
Daybreak unveiled a sweaty, swollen
Stained defeated aftermath cocooned in white sheet

What?
Paralysis?
Is he dead? They all chorused.

His light was out
No more warnings from Mr.Doc
But grandma continues
Serenading the hospital with prayers
Revealing his character layers:

Bless his miserable soul
Pardon his sinful ways
Deliver him now as you did in days of Old

And bring his struggle to a close.
Amen.

A Lover's Wishful Eyes Watching the Tears of a Familiar Sky

On a moody and rainy Day in November
The thought of your smile and laughing eyes
Fill my heart in a trance of cascading memories
With a bleeding heart and weeping Soul
My world takes a turn for a place it knew
A place beyond my feet, kept away by massive watery bodies.
Observing a lizard on a log swirling its tail in the rain
I conclude that what I feel is not real pain;
It is a longing and dryness for my lover's touch
A touch that is familiar and unique.

Surely everything has its season

So on this note I mend my heart
Feeling no regret that we are temporarily a part
For the essence of being is already mapped on a chart
Hence like the lizard I'll swerve dismay from my day;
With the bouncing of my hair.
As I know now that you and I are an infinite pair.

Rocking my love gently in my bosom
My world appeared complete;
Caressing and folding his flesh between lily white sheets…

With the abrupt thundering of the sky

I snapped back to reality
Hands clutching tightly at my own breast
Realizing the casual mental test of life's expected and harsh arrest-

Upon seeing the empty empty face of the space beside me
I exhaled joyfully in the surrounding mountainous fecundity;
Contemplating and reveling in my land to be reunited with thee.
Knowing and believing now

>This is not just "A Lover's Wishful Eyes Watching the Tears of a Familiar Sky."

African Enslavement is largely embodied in the works of many Caribbean writers hence it is not surprising that there is the essence of captivity in this truth as I hold space for those who fought for me to be this free today.

Slave of a Kind

Ring my heart dry, drip it free of all blood
Sweep the ash from my dusty knees
Crushed the pupils free from light
Feed me the dark purpose as agony reels down my cheeks
Cheers to the emissaries of a battered world
Physical blood suckers and mind rattling pricks
Say hai[12] when the knot in my ankles grab and buckle me to the dirt
Face pressed against the source of my birth
Knowing my return, I roared to the sun
Marooned[13] in chaos and spent for death
Only the brightness of his wrath shown to me
Aren't souls to be won for worthiness?
Fooled for the glory of stones and gilt
Stained for grace was the garment modeled
An outfit gift wrapped and custom made
Never were there to be spring in the heart of the fire
Borne of riches are the offspring of virtue
Railed by warmth and laid by mercy
So to the morrows with sorrows from the din
Nowhere special is the destination
Long ranges and short blows each aim bullseye
And fun had the striker who thought he had fun;
words from Pearl are never done.

---

[12] Hai - A vote of agreement; same as yes (as used in the poem Slave of a Kind).
[13] Marooned - Lost/destitute (as used in the poem Slave of a Kind).

Mi Bandana[14]

Mi Bandana from mi mada
Sailors sail is mi Bandana
A country's national flag is mi bandana
A woman's honor is mi Bandana
An anthem for change is mi bandana
A nation's pride is mi bandana
A trophy from warriors' rage is mi Bandana
Mi Bandana, mi bandana is mi Bandana
Bodies wrapped in Bandana moving to the Congo[15]
Wheeling hopelessly for the cause
Feet sole red; fire breaths igniting the wind
Women, men and children
Animal blood mark each palms
Strength of the spirit too strong for the young ones
Each one head hung with shut eyes leaning one onto the other
Red is the night and gray are the mood
What power is in the hands of the puppet master
Dangling fingers on the edge of the Congo
Women huddle closer and men frozen bodies
Set the stance for what to come
The empty, the filled and the halflings
What despair awaits these bodies
Drifted beyond their continent.

---

[14] Bandana - Jamaica's national heritage material used to make traditional clothing often worn as costumes at national events. It used to mean heritage pride (as used in the poem Mi Bandana).
[15] Congo - Place in Africa where the slave trade was primary. Referenced place in the transatlantic slave trade (See poem Mi Bandana).

Into the unknown they disappear.

A country's national flag is mi bandana
A woman's honor is mi Bandana
An anthem for change is mi bandana
A nation's pride is mi bandana
A trophy from warriors' rage is mi Bandana
Mi Bandana, mi bandana is mi Bandana.

From the Lawns

That big old house on Jefferson Street[16]
How could it be more antiquated?
Imagine the queen and king who dwelleth therein
Once upon a time it all was green
Now brown and black is the old timer's plaque.

A frog leapt over seven rocks
Missed the fly for which it traveled
Lolled through the marshy patch
Smacked body flat on the lotus sheet
Drifting aimlessly on ivory green silvery water
A Bigger Forest, thicker trees, a higher vine tower
What more site could it wish to see?

The spider kept its pace
Rolling, lowering spiraling effortlessly in space
Pulling at corners none really see
Boxes and stretchy shapes after it finishes with the endless lace
Where had it caught such designs?
knowing when to measure and end each cut
No fancy seamstress or clever hut.

Under the feared faced moon all shone so flighty
Yet stillness obsolete glows beauty folds
Over the lavender near the bamboo palms high on the oak

---

[16] Jefferson Street - Main street off Broadway in St Louis Missouri.

Northern Mockingbird lull the rushes by the rock
The crackles of dried leaves smashed by the slithering hisser.

A Bigger Forest, thicker trees, a higher vine tower
What more site could it wish to see?

New York Times

One smaddy[17] a nobody fi everybody who don't know a blasted[18] baddy[19]
So, the coffee cups insulation still thin it seems
For if all cups up and no cheers are to throw
Why then must the cup be up more than the very frame next to the cup holder?
Heels gripping pavements and heads arrow forward
Guess the race for the slice of pie is on
Sorry for the merry that dear to tarry or shout
Yoo-hoo hey what's up Harry-
A slice of the apple race is on
Not a morning, howdy doo[20]
Not even a whimsy God bless you
You mean not one of the Lord's people present?

One smaddy a nobody fi everybody who don't know a blasted baddy
Rush hour, car and people all in one accord
Hardworking and all working for the record?
Crush that! screamed jane cheering with the candy filled game
What level are you? a big smile from the two behind
The tube stopped door wide open
Bye, Silly girl said joking

---

[17] Smaddy - Jamaican Patois word for somebody.
[18] Blasted- Jamaican Patois word that translates anger. Usually used as a curse word to show anger or frustration.
[19] Baddy - Jamaican Patois means the human body.
[20] Howdy Doo - Jamaican way of greeting another person.

All heads still looking on phone and tablets smiling and laughing.
This seems different; China Town
Elbows launched a blow to her side
Kid yelled yow watch my device this is a pigi[21]-filled site
No difference in these parts, whether people in bus, cars or pushing carts.

One smaddy a nobody fi everybody who don't know a blasted baddy
Where are the days of smelling the daisies
Pointing at rainbows and feeling crazy
Making love-kisses in streets while kids are giggling
Scream john tom how's d day treating yah[22]
Mary jane asking to hold the coffee cup, searching for stray coins for the beggar
New Rochelle is the modern-day tiger
Every soul to their own; rushing, bumping and straight going
What's the hurry, no-one to admire the first snow flurry
A hunch if it's no beauty in summer to see how will winter conjures any glee?

---

[21] Pigi - Pokémon of the Japanese animated series called Pokemon. A pigi-filled site is the virtual enhancement of a geographical location. Once a player is in the physical location they score.
[22] Yah - Word meaning you.

Bosom Of My Love

Hold me, squeeze me so I need no more
Fill my heart, thrill me so I be dead no more
Where are the fiery eyes to steal my thoughts?
When will the days come that I'll weep rivers no more?
The cedar bend for the pain in me
The willow silenced for the rage from my mouth
Heaven knows the loss of the bosom of my love
Rigorous treacherous hands now hold me
Minds stink of thoughts of me
Faces made to order me
Could there be any of me in the remains of this frailty?
Not one more look at the work I do
How else can I get
When lustier frames appear to be
I sink in the density of my iniquity
Not one feeling of innocence as shame is the style
Garment wasted for its worth none less than a curse
If ever you're asked why must she walk forever long
Whistle to fill the space if never my face has met yours
But if ever yours did tell I miss the bosom of my love.

As a character of power and freedom in the world created in these poems, autonomy and power allows for clarity in scenes as I breathe life into characters, naming them. One could say that I am God-like in this world, crafted by my hands, omniscient and precise in telling stories and my level of knowingness. I only cease this space to reinforce the female of all times and reasonability. Gender and femininity unfold greater issues and for many may be understood as complex characterization while others will conclude diabolism. Confessions of guilt from desires for women to erotic encounters with another woman creates somewhat of a gamble, not knowing how the labels will be thrown. This love affair with this woman is juxtaposed with a deeper desire for political power to cause and effect societal change.

John Tom's Love Letter

Long legged Sheeron Thatcher
Scarlet Butter as you melt away in that chiffon
One sweat trickling from nowhere special
Landing on your nose
Crashing in the softness of your womaness
Tell me how much you love these summer days.
Carnal barbarians scourging the waters of this river boat
Betting all for the givings but never a coin for keeps
All night the balls turn not for matching
Somehow winnings are of another kind.
Tell me Sheeron Thatcher are the good ones here yet?
Perfumed in the sweat of disgrace stolen for grief
Amend command seven for the devil in you overlooked the eighth!
Wound in the hands of time
Craving only the sap of the bark being shredded in this dark
Nothing is left when at last your index pierced this hardback
The covers are off and the paper is out on the table
Must you scrap years of work for minutes play?
Slapping that box make pictures plus number
One less worthy time after time
Pardon for the taunting of this rambler:
Spitting on dices, chancing images aren't my policy-
Prefer snuggled cold winters, making jokes at old fallacy
Humbly clearing a coy brat apparel's more legacy
so no more spreading those cards at high rollers table

making carnival of your colors
nor ShowTime at Grand street corners
simply for I love You of all cheats.

Topics such as politics and capitalism are dealt with as institutions of patriarchy that prevent women progress into positions of power as head of states and seek to highlight women as fragile respectively. The mentioning of politics asks the question of why there are not many female leaders as heads of states? and asks the public to acknowledge that women are not given equal opportunity as men in governance. Capitalism is looked at in the beauty industry. This industry's biggest profit comes through the ideology that women are to look a certain way. This prescription of beauty has given way to a stereotype of how a woman should be in weight, body size, etc. to be seen as beautiful. The concerns of health issues are undertone to ask to what extent should a woman go to pay the price of beauty? The quality of life for the woman is put under the microscope to highlight that there is no uniqueness in a woman where capitalism is concerned, and instead women are seen as mere objects that have no individuality.

Hillary In Line

Who placed her there?
Thousands of nemeses planted there
Origins of races with no traces
The continuum breaks and join in seconds
Bemusing the world of this age
Modernity scuffles for answers to questions unamusing
No science nor founding fathers' lethargic conscience can answer
Rigged in defeat some kneel to the crosses of the ways
Others cling to several Isms and 'self'-righteous cults
Darwin and Freud would be outlaws
none can decipher how is it to be or not to be-
those who are surely changeable nor the dome,
the dome hoisted by so called values and norms
peculiarity seems far uncanny in this world-wind of uncertainties
How does one live unhoused in this house called earth?
What is this that holds the beginnings
And when found, who fits determining these findings?
Who will the mass elect?

Knitting Hands

Never let your right hand knows what the left knows
Fastidious care in these words of old,
But the opposite in knitting and other things I presume
Both hands moving rhythmically to crazy dips and spins
Precise counts and the direction of the needle
Poking into the fabric, manipulating one line to make forms
Similarly there's the lead man in government
Picking at men's brain seeing who is more malleable
Choosing one after the other to create distorted designs.

Hollywood's Poortraits

Cinched waist to the pinched nose
Toy eyes to the plastic rear
Dragged up cheek bones to the anemic frame
Must all the dolls be the same?

All's bright from carpet walks
More like a rug walk where bare walks
Class and purity are forgone to sleazy desperate shows
No more prized than a penny's worth thought.

Why march bare for no cause
An insult to those who stripped to make our kind free to be
To be all that's possible; not limited to made up dolls
Waiting to be dressed and boxed up to go

Slanderous! Slanderous Slanderous
When Endless yards of Royal Red Rug is laid out
Ancient rituals for Esteemed Royals,
But, "in-come" body parts and full body displays
Mothers, and grandmothers alike braving morality
All to show, who to show, the nothings to show?

Her music is empty as she fills the videos scantily
All the wastes in the minds, fills in pasted silly
Hypocrites chatter her details and are consumed in her scents

For after show in one's secret confines, her melodies make the world gay.

To The Heaven from Sorrow

Cheer up good times
Happy Dreams and sweetness chimes
Up to heaven your prayer climbs
How sweet I feel writing these lines
Keep cherry and merry
Singing and smiling with the Promised Ferry
The Day when fresh air is yours to keep
And the past will be in sand so deep.

The Colors in Me to The World Out There

Stolen hearts;
Chapped feet
And backs against a whitewashed wall.
Out in the open the sun ripened
I paired my back from the clouded mess
Stained shirt and bruised skin were the days dress
Shower time;
The tainted shirt had imprinted onto me
Mirror showed only teeth truly white
My nappy mop spiked to its full height
My fiery eyes intensified its light
A fist balled into its full might
I crashed it into the mirror
Blood mixed splinters show my error
I screamed with a white-faced interior
Wronged;
In then numbness of my soul
Green when the day's dirt stick to my skin
Blue when hurt makes me dim
Yellow when my brave is slim
All these color I am,
Whenever;
But Black I'll always be
No more I'll tone my dark

Perm[23] isn't a criterion for Noah's Ark
To be in real is my new start.

---

[23] Perm - Chemical treatment used to refine hair texture (as used in the poem The Colors in Me to the World Out There).

Black Seeds of Ferguson St. Louis 2014

My Mother's seed are scattered on barren soil
Little fruits to be choked on thorny ground
Half-grown trees hacked from the limbs down
Rarely are the fruits grown to lay at the mother tree's feet.

Flashing dancing streetlights
Dark cold haunting allies and parks
All the scenes are one;
Whether light or dark
They heard the cry and none to say
They saw the butcher and covered their face.

Morning raised her skirt
And the spoils from the night's raid are shown
Another of my mother's seed;
A fallen berry strayed to corner street
Dark juices crusted his figure to asphalt
Not a fire hose can wash the scene afresh
Detectives scribble question marks in their book of query.

Other bearers gathered feeding;
One with a little cherry
Her lips smothered and caressed it
He isn't safe although fastened waist high
For his mother's womb is an open wound
An ancient canvas drenched

Of only bruises of her painters' brush
So, Ferguson is the unseen treaty
The wretched reapers Cree.

A Man's Wife and Life to Take
'The Husband's Tale'

Heard of words from "Still I Rise"
And stories of the Woman who stood her ground,
Preferably held her seat,
Tales from Greek Mythology of Zeus[24] and Athena[25],
Fables from Arabian Nights and the boy with his magical
Carpet,
Editions from the Prince who woke the princess,
Nursery Rhymes of the fragile one who sat on the wall
Cherished classics of the Victorian and Elizabethan ladies
and Lords,
And the Eroticas of deserted housewives and thirsty
men…
How about your story?
Tell me of your pirate ship or adventures saving lives,
Was it a raging night that ceased the light of your eyes?
Could it be in your steward flight you stole dangers way
Freeing a random damsel?

Any news would soothe this freelancing goon,
A plea for sweet words
Coated with a more pungent reality.
This shark good eyed him in The One Stop

---

[24] Zeus - The Supreme God of ancient Greece (as used in the poem A Man's Wife and Life to Take, The Husband's Tale).
[25] Athena - As used in the poem "A Man's Wife and Life to Take; The Husband's Tale". In Greek mythology, she is the Goddess of War.

He has the shakes[26]
Wrestling a lighter from his coat chest
Even the darkest corner wanted his tory[27] told-
One clumsy move and there
Silver steel kissed his waist,
As the coat lay open
Blood-soaked rag pinned his leg.

He jolted at the sirens
And his hands betrayed the gins bottle
Shattered glasses screamed at him
He covered his ears
The valentine color of the ambulance
Danced with the pub's Disco lights
Oh, what a scene
Sam drowned in regrets; worse of all his guilts,
Shouted in the barrel of his gun;
"My wife and my life to take"
When it growled back at him
The room leveled in silence
And night became longer than ever.

---

[26] Shakes - used to mean an uncontrollable nervousness, like the nervousness displayed in addicts. (as used in the poem A Man's Wife and Life to Take, The Husband's Tale).
[27] His Tory - stories that are meant to look good but not necessarily be factual (as used in the poem "Voice from the Oceans Floor for Ben Solomon Carson").

Heart Of the Brain

Dreaming with open eyes and busy mind
Memories wild, some very vague
Washed ashore by a longing feeling
Accompanied by the resounding Titanic's tune
Marinating my thoughts and digging at my heart
The heart who no longer feels
I say this; from its path blood is barred
Leaving a well-defined shell
A shell which offers no storage

Far too long have I listened to you
Now I'll go by directions of the brain
It will not render me anymore pain
Strange is life and strange are the ways of men.

Gazing bright eyed through the dark
A noticeable lonely long light pole
Stood crooked necked with its pendant lightly hanging
Carelessly it blinked casting shadows about;
Terrifying angry shadows with claws and extended incisors
Often lovers linger turns lurid mingling under this backdrop of overcast.

An Arousal of The Long Forgotten

Upon the high where a rock's head was finally released
Watching a bloody sun sunk into the midst of a calm blue sea
She realized how dangerous a love can be

For he so loved the world he gave his precious lamb to slaughter

Green hats laid upon earth mounds
Now calmer was the wind
Her heart felt for such a love to many unknown
The sight within this field of maize is unforgotten
With shards of barely against oily overworked skin
Beads of sweat climbed layers of muscles landing everywhere on nowhere
Is this the passion of Christ or devil's lustfulness?

One will never be sure
For who will ever know
The sweetness of the treasures she had found
Bare, wasted and still betrothed
The morrow bring Easter Day and it shall ring her white day bells
Feast to join two families and a bride pure and detailed as ocean shells
Well at least that's the tale she forever tells.

At times feeling victimized by societal stereotypes, my surreptitious mind breaks its code to plead the fifth and free will wins creating a quickening to escape the boxes of marginalization that society has laid as traps. Feel with me as empathy is sought for those who suffer among us, whether it be emotional turmoil, ailment, or the extremities of death. Through voice, activism for minorities is potent, specifically on matters of race, diversity, and inclusivity. My duplicitousness in being an Afro Caribbean and African descent in foreign America adds richness to the commentaries on race being a factor in people who have lost their lives, a premise for individuals to be deprived of certain quality of life and the foundation of the larger picture of discrimination that forms systematic oppression of a particular race of people.

Voices from the Ocean's Floor for Ben Solomon Carson[28]

Don't look for thee in old history
It's lies and hi-story
Search in the bricks of old towns
My brother's father's uncle, and sons made those squares
Look under ancient sugar house boilers
It was the grave for many unfortunate toilers

Why is my brother lost to show?
How could a brain surgeon's head possess such awful woe?
Where is the wise in this Solomon?
When did you become an how- man?

---

[28] Ben Solomon Carson - His full name is Benjamin Solomon Carson, Retired Neurosurgeon in America. He was appointed as the Secretary of Housing and Urban Development. He was depicted as very controversial at some point.

Street Talk of Immigrants in Glee
"America's Run for Greatness 2016"

Brave the night to see the stars
Challenge the days to whisper loudly

Hardbound Hearts torn in defeat
Has the mighty gone from our kind?
What great fall is to come?
If his map is only for some?
How a race is great when faulty is the race?

Torrents of Black Pride Rebel
Synchronized Muslim fears turn to hate
Egotistical mendacious villains wage mainstream wars
What tyrant unleashed such dreads?
Walls for the maybe saved runaway victims
His presence commanded only Sieg Heil[29]
Oh this he hadn't been deprived
Once golden hands now bore tarnished metal

God forsaken mutt,
German bulldog with English foxhound
Amateurism in the greatest house ever built
A blaspheme to the forefathers
An unconscionable baboon wielding power as if its bananas and filth.

---

[29] Sieg Heil - Nazi salute gesture used at political rallies (as used in the poem Street Talk of Immigrants in Glee; America's Run for Greatness 2016).

Despair and confusion sit atop the hill
Chauvinism bolded a chance to democracy
Shared fear and need for change in the aristocracy
Revered New World labeled "shortened greatness"
Make America great again; hypocrisy
The new media stifled in bureaucracy
Pastors prayed to the Ancient
All faces turned toward the hill
From there all needs should be fulfil!

Bow to the risen sun

Only then will this craze be done.

The Move

Clueless days and never-ending nights
Tight fitted trunks; carrier of her burdens
Cobwebs stretched across her hot pink heels
Who to wear them when the occasions grew a few
No more summer days with Kool aid stands,
Barbecue smell stained shirts,
Long gone are the dessert weekends and smoke buddy t-shirts
Who will drink the green blends and cheer with celery sticks?

Maybe the Spring will give her a new ring
Open her lawns with daffodils, and bloomed green bushes
What sudden change stole her rhythm?
Bare to the core
No more inpatient honk from a horn,
Not when her drive-way and street side has spell-bound vacancy
Lone time TV dinners will rot her mind I fancy.

What joy can a single photo offer?
That brother is caged from her world.
Someone tell Jenny he's not worth her penny
One look through those windows and love you'll see
For my father awaits thee
Open to his light and shame that dark
Poor Jenny let not sin be your final mark.

For Josephine

Hell is no place for a queen
Look! the mirror never lies
There's a crown for all to see
Raise your faith to the heavens
Show the soul you know
Rattle the ground with stumps
Shake the walls of slumber low
Shout the truth for the hills and towers to reach
It is not fallacy that was preached
Revelations of the hearts and affirmation in the eyes
Can you deny, there's none as this wonder we seek?
None to baffle our earthly sight
None to conjure company in loneliness
Only this One send the thrills that tremble the body,
Set fire to the tongue that once only tasted,
And transformed the wretch that never belonged.
Come go forth and walk the seas,
Fly the plains and tell of the great deeds,
Write the people of the World,
Set the evidence in magazines and talk shows:
How all would listen and fanned the fields clean of the crows
Make sense save the grains to lessen the foes.

Tender Flesh
(Our mothers who mothered in Secret)

Tender flesh Nanny
What a sweetness is our Annie
Thought you were alone?
That milk you gave David never left the memory
That look you gave him told me he wasn't of me.

And when her dark arms overlapped his pale skin
His steel blue eyes searched her face and relaxed under the lids
One clung to her chest the other at play on the floor
Tears kept to the back of her eyes and she placed the babe in his carriage
Afraid to show they are of her
She whisked away to water the patios fern
Never said a word to Madame but was satisfied in her secret mother's pride.

Simple Life

Simple things are worth the frenzy[30]
Simple things created the larger picture out there
The mansions, great travels and fancy cars aren't all
Simple things made the laughs and tender smiles
Grand paintings created awe of its simple makings
Fine sculptures dynamics are formed from simple mimics
Walks in the park, Green grass picnics,
Fishing by the lake, riding St. Louis arch
Sunday Church and Friday night beers
These Simple things are worth champagne cheers.

---

[30] Frenzy - Means to celebrate (as used in the poem Simple Life).

Home Away from Home

Several times she called
Late nights and bright mornings
Several times she called
Busy days and blue afternoons
Several times she called.......

Not a picture but blurred is the face once known
Her voice was distant but the love pulled me near
Something worried her, something dark was the fear
The height in the tone told her days of lone
And her cry dear daughter do not leave the phone
How the sadness in me screamed
With hell in my heart I heard it all

Several times she called
Late nights and bright mornings
Several times she called
Busy days and blue afternoons
Several times she called......

When the hangover stopped its always another night
No worry, no haste to be anywhere
When yesterday's portion hurled from my chest
Still I made time for Jack Daniel's pint
Turned reality into a great fantasy
Somehow, I made it to Tennessee
Drank and shook hands with Jack Daniel's Former Family

Several times she called
Late nights and bright mornings
Several times she called
Busy days and blue afternoons
Several times she called......

On The Day of Pentecost

Pinned in Pentecost
Unworthy prize I am for the grand cost
Oh what lethargic hearts could do
The fire of the core is never sore
The Blazed Being that quickens for sure
Ever about somewhere out there
It knows of all the secret ways
It hovers for all the saints' days

Oh, may I look upon his face
Touched his garment of pure
Astounded by the glorious Wonder
Be comforted in eternal glee
Dragged from the damned;
The mark the beast has set upon the earth
For the rapture, I'll dream to be forever free.

Grandpa's Radio

Played a tune that dispelled doom
Merged a rhyme that defies time
Show me unreals that narrowed my eyes
Sunk me deep in the unknowns.

I long for Samson's strength and Solomon's wits
I bare the burdens of my mother
I pray her strength beguile my limbs
Fortified they'll be my columns
This building is young but bears the scars of old quakes.

Play a tune to call my mothers
Merge a rhyme transcending space
Show the truth to fever my eyes
Lay me gently on the shallows.

Alexander's song mellowed my ears
Shredded countless heartbreaks
Bandaged distant mourns
And journey my Pa's soul over Atlantics to the land of the free.

Imagine If I Tried

Ten toes I counted at once
Ten fingers I measured at once
Squirming and yelling she came
Pains and strains I thought of not
Little devil I see her full
Strange the sound that caved my nerves
Busy doing nothing she wailed and wailed
Wide mouth and awkward moves
This bundle my world it shall steal
Deep inside I found it unreal
On the surface another task I see
Somewhere out there another understands
The pain, the joy, the not-knowingness that gleams
This fool cooing at my pain and test to be
"Pretty little joy" was the day's title
Underline subtitle read, work and thoughts to sort
Drained and accomplished, the feelings I emitted
Yet who cares when here lies the most of beauties to see.

The Joy I Bled

Kinsmen[31] from the market days
Was it size, ripeness or seasons that made the pick?
They weren't like jewels so the value would in carats appraised
They weren't like fruits so the readiness would in quality appraised
They weren't like animals so the breed would in kind be appraised
They weren't like art so the work would by artiste be appraised
They weren't like wine so the date would in year be appraised
They weren't like plants so the exoticism in species would be appraised?

How could man see his own features and lay it to nothingness?
Outdoors and wild fields to toil and dwell
Offspring to pluck distort and shipped afar
On the world's market my kinsmen were priced

Man dirtied his own image for profit
Privileged today in the name of greed
while 'Others sweat under steal blue skies
Kinsmen from the market days
Strength are seen in old brick walls
Names are etched in history's holidays;

---
[31] Kinsmen - A relative.

Immortalized, thee for many today, tomorrow and yesterdays joy that I bled.

The Yellow Tail That Never Sings

Mangled faces keep my sleep afar
Shrinking laughter creep into my ears
Faint scents gallop past my nose
Fragments of home lay me waste

Yellow tail keeps me afloat
The bird that never sings
Its color gives no myriad of delights
I entertain its presence because its most affordable
When it fills me entirely, I slumber everlastingly.
Oh, bird of my own make
I wonder how I'd see if you were never to be;
Music only I hear
shows you give when my shutters are down
Belongingness when alien is the label, I wear
The stronger your presence, the weaker I feel
One would fail to appreciate the comfort you exude to me; an expatriate.

In the many mirrors of life, I witness the journey traveled by women across time and space, reflecting various aspects of voice, tone, and experiences. I, Josephine, is a timeless and global character in my own right, a record keeper, and almost a historian. My purpose is to present history timelessly, ensuring that important events such as political election tensions, social and civil unrest, prejudice, and discrimination are highlighted. These misfortunes serve as points of reflection, from which we can learn, empathize, and create avenues for all of humanity to improve. With this improvement, we fulfill our duty of allyship for the greatest. We can fulfill our duty of allyship for the greatest good.

For The Brevity of Sowore; Brother from My Mothers Land

Tell me story of days gone and ones to come
Where the fowled ones are bare to truth
Prisoner of the revolution
Man, like Omoyele Sowore[32]
Founder of Sahara Reporters
Today a common criminal
Fugitive of words arbitrary they say
Shoveled piled and caged his pay
Muzzled cornered and violated beyond a day

Soyenka!
Laureates of our times
Dissected and cleared the real
Still the words held a giant restraint
Is it the words or men's heart his constraints?
History played back as in times of Mandela
The people against the people for the people

The twists of dying soles placed to lead life
Unread brains set to write laws
Bare gums dare to chew bones
Spineless men hands at the base of a nation
Blind eyes made to look at light
The paraplegic set to race down the straight

---

[32] Omoyele Sowore - Nigerian human rights activist who was arrested in August 2019 in his activism protest.

Tell me story of days gone and ones to come
Where the fowled ones are bare to truth
Pride set ablaze honor
Arthritis full a knee of honor
Frail framed bent the back to which custom clamor
Tell me man of yesterday won't you respect the life of tomorrow?

Body Politics

Nothing mere about me
Nothing random about me
Not just anyone can be me
I breathe life incubated in the dark of light
I sustain bodies from the substance I am
I keep grown men in tune
Centering their minds, finance and socioemotional frame

Throw my wig on a broom
Fling my dress on a frame
Dash my heels on a crook stick
Drag my makeup on pavements
Haul my corset onto a dummy
Flash my attitude on billboards
Stick my perfume on stench
Clip my bras on a donkey
Pin my pants on a baboon

Anything to discredit me
Anything to redefine me
Anything to destabilize me
Anything to minimize me
Anything to discourage me from being me

Rethink your how to slow me
Rethink your acts to box me
Rethink your way to slay me
Rethink your aim to claim me

Rethink your plan to shame me
Rethink how you show the show you show.

Gberemene[33] George Floyd of my Father's Land

The dead who sounded the Abeng
I've seen many in Maroon Town
Young muscles whose mouth made no sound
Elders laughed and said young man you don't have the power
Maroons if the Ashanti said its power to blow,
The Abeng; blown only by powerful men
A belief debunked
He was Royal; George Floyd was his name
A dead man sounded the Abeng
Belated the rhythm of the dead; young and old
Nations woke; the dead and living in unison
We heard you pikin[34] from our dust
He summoned his mother
And Pa-Yoma[35] answered him
Open arms, Pa-tete[36] erected and wide eyed
On his knee with lowered head they greeted;
Mkana Mone[37]! George son of the earth
And when Ra[38] kissed his face, he smiled
Ovele ba do[39] seed of the blessed fruit.

---

[33] Gberemene - Nigerian Ogoni tribe language meaning High King.
[34] Pikin- Nigerian Ogoni language word meaning Child.
[35] Pa-Yoma - Nigerian Ogoni language word meaning ancestral spirits.
[36] Pa-tete - The one you need.
[37] Mkana Mone- Nigerian Ogoni language word meaning I greet you.
[38] Ra - Name for the Egyptian sun God with a bird head.
[39] Ovele Ba Do - You came quicker.

George answered I was never meant to grow old
They will remember me young
I'll be the one who was never done
Continued from today and ends when tomorrow is no more
Born to man; purposed for the God above
This I know for my Father's book show this as footnote
Flesh I was but spirited even greater.
The message we know was encoded in "Mama"
The word that shook heaven and rented the earth
Floyd:
Father, Son, Uncle, brother, cousin and lover
All the natural title of a common man
Look harder and you will see:
Gberemene Royal Blood from my Father's Land
You killed a King and his blood ignite fire
Races torn, borders broken and the world became still;
Trapped in the trance of intense in that instance.

His mother didn't answer
The Line of Yoma heard his call
Ose do[40] pikin from our dust.

---

[40] Ose Do - Nigerian Ogoni language word meaning welcome.

Minnesota Protests

Black bodies in unforeseen state of emergency
People screamed I can't breathe;
ready black man's insurgency
Calls from the left, answers from the right
Uneasiness in between
Liberals and conservatives have no rhass[41] answer
Still in admittance to the imbalanced scales they use to measure
Feelings got high; tones became deafening to the cry of why?
Stop, look, listen and engage the man for the injustice
Forget the so-called unity, be true to the law
The one that says shackle man no more
Let him master his own affairs
Let his work be his own to profit from
His family now his to manage
Clear laws served consistently is the only answer, one America.

---

[41] Rhass - Jamaican curse word. Same as the "F" word.

Africans in Motion: From Plantations to Boulevards

Old news today's headlines
Dr. Martin Luther King; paved the way to march
Frederick Douglas; brevity in his harsh remarks

From the bassinet to the grave
Valleys to mountainside
Land to seas outstretched
Through barren sands to lushness of green
On earth ascends to the heavens great blue
In the silence of the abyss to the cries beyond
In slumbers set deep to the wake of souls
Over plains to the dip of gullies
Grace, triumph, jezebels and lost wars
Fears tossed aside to address the cares of the world
Wails, smiles of joy all forged the work to jubilee
I curtesy in cross lanes with pride dashed aside
All give way to escorted black freedom vigils in the street
Afro Indo Asian, yellow, black, red and all the colors in the rainbow
Behold bitter head arrows bore brothers today
And from their mouth came venoms
Blood shone from their eyes
And their salted skin thronged the sung arched roads.

Grey Thoughts in the Black Abyss

In a place of new horizons and dreams in multitudes
They too are lost and dig in deep caves of the past
Whole testimony on old days captured through lenses
People scourging the books of history
Clinging to black and white photos and converting their name to mean much More;
Whether Afrikaan, mere biblical, Egyptian or Moore
A first world modeling drags, rags - the people drag

Brothers, fathers, uncles -Men
Sisters, mothers, aunts-Women
Stand, March, Shout, and Rebel
Vices of a system broken, and candy coated; red and blue-
The dye no longer dry, bled and the base cane showed white;
White as snow and bare to all to see.
Fearless they confronted the disease of 2020,
Pandemic secondary to the racial epidemic
Old Hatred molested their freedom-
Flung open doors and landed them mute,
In day, chase them with cars and cuff them - many dead,
At night chase them and God knows the end.

Say their names, the slogan that matters!

Learn their names, for the hooligans to whom nothing mattered!
Remember their names, to the allies decided and the somewhat armatures.
Hear their names, for the world to tout their immortal beauty in various artistic caricatures!
For these are the names that will determine your children's names.

Year 2021 and my mothers' cry from old scorns
She said no more and not on my time
She felt a man attack her peace and freedom she now mourns.

Section II

The common themes of entrapment, the desire to be free, slavery and the experience of the many facets of life through the woman's eyes are the common repetitive themes throughout Josephine in the Mirror, as the readers move through the many dimensions illustrated by the single character Josephine. The anthology serves almost as a bildungsroman categorically as the single main character Josephine is frozen in time in Section II in comparison to her agelessness and timelessness in a geography that stretched from the Caribbean to the American soil in Section I. Here my life and world is in a fixed time; year 2020-2022 with my expressions of thoughts on issues of politics, race, and gender, that are present day issues. Fixated in time, still does not provide the freedom to evoke the vestiges of slavery to explain the status of reality. The backdrop of today's America are hints of weaknesses and strengths that go together to materialize both the palatable and distasteful features of the moment, however nonetheless my appetite for this new space is unchanged regardless of this sweet-sour world that is destined for change. A change that freely occurs and, in some instances, demanded by force of the minorities. Consciousness of wokeness[42] is paramount and is the single factor that links my Caribbean roots in Section II.

---

[42] Wokeness - Being aware of African-ness or what it entails to be Black. Quite often referring to the structures that Persons of African Descent struggles with in American society.

The Colonizers – Abatement of Xamaca

Bare, open; waiting a land in the middle of the Caribbean Sea
Lush vegetation, it's soil grows anything that's buried in it
And when night comes its world is lit by sounds of all sorts
Often, they say one can hear ghosts or see water mama combing her locks on moonlit rocks
Its fruits wild and their deep red or golden skins will pour you juice endlessly
Up its mountain's coffees, chocolate, astonishing floras and butterflies dance to chirp chirps and the whooshing wind
Relics from Bacra[43] aid in the beauties and are backdrops to his century's plunders
Who am I to tell you of bushes that feeds mangoes, apples and wild plums
Who am I to tell you of river white stones sharpened to scale our fishes
Who am I to tell you of big gum trees with swinging vines
Who am I to tell you of bauxite soil red that goes on and on for miles
Who am I to tell you of people who move their bodies to strange beats:
Beats that summoned years of pain
Gyrations that flung the stress of hardship and poverty somewhere, nowhere that is mapped

---

[43] Bacra/Bacra Massa- Name in Patois for a slave master. Used in modern Jamaica to speak of the government. One common term with this word is Bacra Pickney, which means that a child belongs to the government, so one is answerable to the law for harming a child.

Who am I to tell you that the green the gold and black are to fend your attack
To spirit these souls to a newfound owned and free ambiance
Regardless of your rage, rape, onslaught, greed, misguided appetite
Today's legacies are from yesterday's careless excursions
So, little is the ask of today.

To My Country's Queen Elizabeth II
(Ghost of My Promised Land)

Howdy your royal highness
I've watched you all my life of thirty
Names of grace, purity, and strength armor you
From coronation days to present days ordained they said is your reign
You appear delicate, proper and with unwavering moral
I've seen you blessed in your simple plain dress
Precious jewels set aside and canopy separated you from public's eyes
The Pope himself overseen your precious frame
And invoke the Holy Spirit on your special day.

Howdy your royal highness
I've watched you all my life of thirty
Names of grace, purity, and strength armor you
Is it softness I see in your eyes?
Is it courage that glues you to the media?
Is it your heart of gold that keeps your hand outstretched with that gloved effortless waive?
Your life of collecting curtsies, praises and right choice broach for events;
Your families' traditions of passing tiaras, titles and special events in spaces shared
By predecessors are noteworthy
Impeccable traditions; very important
British media and cousins in the West
All of these they hold in high esteem.

Howdy your royal highness
I've watched you all my life of thirty
Names of grace, purity, and strength armor you
With days passing, deaths are inevitably looming
Today's strife and long awaiting ascensions
Murmurs and contentious deliberations
Who's next; befitting, complete in political suave,
Public diplomacy to keep the heart of the world affixed to
royal glory?
Little ones pranced on lawns
Middle ones show prowess in sports and display party
galivants
Older ones raised brows and advertised correctness of
traditions.
How upright, fragile yet strong.

Howdy my queen
All my hurts, are my country's sore
All my tears are my country's sweat
All my hunger is my country's famine
All my needs are my country's emptiness
All my not having is my country's poverty
Brain drains of the best minds
All my kinsmen global wanderings are from who is next in
your line?
May God save the Queen.
Or perhaps not.

For When the Son of Men Shall Stand

For when at the fork I twist
For when in the midst of the road undecided
For when the hostile chose tempering their temper
For when the shrouds are cleared
For when the markers are erased
For when the dark is whitened
For when the dirt removed show pure
For when the diamonds are no longer in the rough
For when the lilies are not knife scorched under the sun
For when the sheep are safe from the wolves
For when the ugly is transformed beauty
For when the storms are ceased
For when the earth is no more wicked
For when our time is pulled to the end
All our sins will be ours to carry
And if the scales are out of balance
To the dust we go from where we came
To bottomless pits we'll drag our hearts
Do the most to bind times hands in the sands
Do the most to share in the wine and bread of life
Do the most to elevate thy neighbor and abort strife.

Highness Mama Tell Jesse Mi Coming Home

Mama tell Jesse Mi coming home
Tell Uncle Sam the daughter returned from across the sea
Prepare the feast and set the white rum
Prepare the bed and clear the shed
All the neighbors, friends and far out family with hands outstretched

Who wants scented candles, sweet soap, candy cane and a dollar from Merica.
All the spoils I bring ashore
All this while my bones ache to rest in island mineral bath
Mouth went wet then dry for sun baked fruits

Nerves are bad now Margie cry
All sort of Rhitis the doc said
I laughed and kissed the old croaks cheeks
Wrinkles overlapped the spot I peeled my lips from
Oh what a journey life is;
The sighing of my heart when I stole my arms from her weak frame
This hug was different from previous ones
It revealed all bones under her big wide frock
This time I reached but soon I know she will leave
No, not anywhere among the journey of the living
Yes I see death in her small beady sunken eyes
And her less wordy pursed lips; just there on her face.

This One was once fire
Always making bonfires and spitting stories to curse all the old ones
Calling names from neons ago
Chastising the idle males and scolding the girls who gave them time
Young women crossed their legs at her presence and young men wore shirts to cover greasy chests when Margie towered over their beings in the yard
Under that very shed,
Now it's the stage to set her rocking chair so she looks on,
Wordless and almost motionless
A little smile here and there to the limitations of her hand wave
Hypnotized by the sun she would lower her head
And fast asleep for a quick half hour
Up again when kids would scream or cry
Now bothered by any rattling she motions to be wheeled in from the shed
All the way to her bed and there she is set down to be rested.
How brutal is time:
Twisting one's body like gum under the sun
Laying waste to man's Vigor and unleaded stamina
How wicked are the hands of time
Punishing a soul once so spirited,
At least now it has where the trimmings stopped from its beginnings.

Wig Wearing Magistrates-Pass the Crown

(For Princess Nzinga[44])

When a black man turn up he is somewhat of a smooth walker, silent talker, Game day announcer
Confusion these brothers, wouldn't you agree?
He is straight back, sometimes almost gliding on earth, straight faced and bwoi[45] when he smiles
Moms are relieved, daughters celebrated and women of all sorts and colors are intrigued
Intrigued for this animal is big, breathtaking, strong and oooh whew! when he flashes his locks
Complete by God, looking like he was chiseled by Zeus on Athen[46]
Finished when he showed up yet, here you are seeing him unkempt and dashed
When Niah[47] touch road, politicians scorn the very ground
When Niah chant, Pastors declared the blood of Jesus is turned
When Niah spit knowledge all admit he's mad
When Niah feet go bare, they call him cheap
When Niah meditates mountains high, they announce him completely mad

---

[44] Princess Nzinga Candace King- Jamaican 16-year-old female Rastafarian whose locks were trimmed by police officers while in police custody on July 22, 2021 in Jamaica.
[45] Bwoi- In Patois means boy or is used and an exclamation of surprise; Bwoi!
[46] Athen-Place in Greece.
[47] Niah-Patois for Rastafarian.

When Niah bashes the Trenton[48], Adventist smile
When Niah glorifies the herb, Doctors research and agree
When Niah says fire to Babylon, the coroner will measure his final degree.

---

[48] Trenton - Patois for Pig meat.

The decadence of Jamaica's morality frothed with colonial residues that seeks to oppress its present-day Jamaican citizens are juxtaposed to American modern day ongoing racial inequity that ran rife in its society and has caused what is referred to as systematic oppression at present. As a self-professed historian I present my two countries (Jamaica and USA) politics as a vehicle that transports individuals' destiny to higher heights or to the opposite hell. Josephine's strength is loud to all, courageously calls for change, with questions raised about how political interests in other countries have united political figures which results in no opposition to mass spending bills, in a time when Ukraine and Russia are at war.

Annie B: A Life Severed Too Soon

Weeping, wailing and gnashing of teeth echoes from my granny's days
Suffering, streams of goose pimples and yanked at my heart on September's 5th
A woman of all heart found with severed throat
Another of my country men, couldn't be more ill of womankind
Tell who among us gentle souls void of a soul?
Who among us took life from our nana's bosom?
Who among us unmoved by the pains of our own bellies?
And if a barren one was among our clan
Death be unto that cold creature
But no,
Evidence haven't revealed Mr. John Doe
So, for now his hell is unatoned
Officers shuffled back and forth
Eagle eyed the gathering
Bagged the dagger found aside her flesh
Officer looked in the mirror of the blood and declared the killer is here
What did the mirror show there?
As if that wasn't enough, he noted no forcible entry
Which friend transformed into this gentile foe?
Clipped the wings of that angel of death
No business he had to approach her close ranged
No duties in hell included a woman of God
And if he challenged this notion
Send that horned creature to space beyond our galaxy

Well, the rich trod the outer borders of planet now
So, to the moon he may be led
But there would be one to pay his jet back
In an instance he would appear as quick as he defaced the
scene from which he fled.

The Deaf Tone of Politics

Funneled fame on campaign when the mass rallies
Open mikes for the future ruler
Controversies of feelings and what he actually can do
Limelight, hand claps and red cheeked infants await his kiss
Talks of freedom to live and the need to cast a vote.

Where will living commence?
Far left, Far right, Liberal or the conservatists
All angles are up for grabs
But the choice must be made amidst the discontent
For the need is great, the stakes are high
The reality will cast the doubts, but the fight is for the right
In the rush of it all
No one noted his idiosyncrasies to be right,
Tales of the boy who cried wolf,
The Emperor's New Suit
The best solution he finds, a game of golf.
Is the blame the painter for the color saturation?
Is the blame the contractor who bid the painter in this nomination?
Surely, expressionism[49] nor fauvism are his admonition
Nonetheless his quickness to paint reality leaves residues of careless designs
We, the people are to cast votes of logic in sound minds
For the choice must be made amidst the discontent
For the need is great, the stakes are high

---

[49] Expressionism- Style of music, painting, and drama in which the artiste expresses emotional experiences instead of the impressions of the external world.

And for the seriousness of the choice
One must not be lead by ini Minnie mini mo, red orange or indigo.

The Fight of The Cousins; White Power

Old movies; Mary Queen of Scots
The Cousin that seeks to dethrone the other
The coldness of attitudes and the fire of wicked desires
Thoughts of people as pawns to aristocrat endless desires
Big screen hits, tales of historical fits and Broadway classical hits
The realities of WWIII on February 24th reeked the globe
Ukrainians faces in tears,
Innocent bodies gummed to the ground
Putin Special Military operation; laid flesh by the pound
People scattered, lives snatched from infants and a society no more
Boys turned Men, drafted themselves, bear arms for the cause

And the agenda; demilitarization and denazification
Of What is asked?
Simple folks, living, loving and being as any other
Atomic weaponry, world domain was never their bother
So, in shambles they make-do and prayed,
while Russia in their lands unconscionably forayed

By then millions worth of aid to the needy
Global frantic spurred and feelings erupted
Patrons across the planet gave hands of all sorts to afflicted
The pandemic postponed so the U.S border could receive
Humane hearts opened their homes to strangers distressed

News appeals showed families welcomed in converted living rooms
They came into jobs and aids of all kinds
The need is there, and the pain globally felt
The question deep with rustling in the gut
Of all the times in the blackest of hurts
why haven't government eagerly exercised similar joy to immigration influx?

Black Girl: Corporate Commodity of Commerce

Clear as day, so confident and high, If I may
Just another day coming in to start the day
It was by Winter's Time
And I felt like Jazz warming the time
My hair a fluffed Winter's Fro
Lips popped with delicate pink
Neck clutched in butterflied scarf
Big sunshine smile that tore the veil of snow
When down to the floor I sank
Mid air one leg right angled and the other reached for the East
That slip sent my back crouched and tears streamed
The scream lowered in my throat
Finally, the yell raptured through Newstead
All the eyes from nowhere on me
Security peeled me from the iced concrete
Up my body hit with aches between my thighs
Through the day my leg prismed its colors
Swollen pink, red then finally purpled
And when the plum burnt so bad the aches fired through my being
Next day spams like current streamed my body
My back and loins all heavy
Tears gripped my eyes, and I felt my strength swayed like levy

The good years and great work by all remarked
You would think they saw me, my humanity
When human resource reprimanded my body
Shut! My senses shrunk and the wall grew higher and thicker
I was nothing but a commodity of Commerce
They saw me not
They heard me not
They felt for me not
When ordered to come back I asked for transportation
Then silenced by the labor laws they drew on
Then denied transportation for my back was completely out
In my space I crawled
In my head I went
In my mirror I saw nobody
In the blank reflection and silencing of Corporate bullying I saw them,
The women of the plantation,
Overworked, beaten, maimed, raped, and left for dead

I said no! order me not
Attend to my pains for you gave me eternal ache
Make my time worthy that I have given to you
Understand that I am flesh and blood as you are
Will your hearts to see me and feel that I bleed
And when tumultuous pain rocked my back
Bent I felt the ground was my equal

In and out to Doctors I went
Back and forth the days starts with medicine and as such it ended
Emailed; pleas and begs were the friends entrusted to deal my means to all ends this financial institution dealt me a wound I'll never forget
Denied my pleas for Doctors at first
Revered themselves as keepers of equity
Pioneering diversity and sustainers of inclusion
Even as alms to such resource groups
I was made to feel the shrunkeness in measurement of my race
Again, I felt me in that small space,
The box I ticked when asked how I identify
I was black, something even dirty defy
I was an alien, something that is not specify
I was neither here nor there
For to me
To be mistreated for a fall at work;
Mauled by Commerce Human Resource Hounds
Showed that I was an abandoned mule with flesh worth less than a pound.

The polarization of America's willingness to help Ukrainians and Congress crawl for internal spending budgets to improve family lives on the Homefront are among topics such as rights to citizenship, xenophobia, colonial neurosis, reparation, that affects the common man and immigrants alike in America. Notably, I'm a figure of free will, yet my choice is to exist as a product of my ancestral legacies, where all observations and emotions are carried through experiences in a system that revolts against an existing oppression.

Caravans Of Ukranian Refugees: They Call Them by Their Nationality; Ukranians

Like crane lift they're delicately carried
Like with feathers to get their back well pat
Like eggs they are handled with much care
Like the shepherds herd they're tended
Like the chosen they are specially gifted
Like humans they're given abundant empathy
Like the race that's for the system they're given space
Like people they are treated
Unto this flock the border is loosened
Over their skins blankets are thrown

And was this in the midst of the pandemic
What pandemic?
News reported policies relaxed to admit them
Resources disbursed to admit them all
Society activated through media streams
They called them by their nationality, Ukranians
Yes, not mediocre claims of caravans, not influx of refugees
No problem from shit hole countries
Every blasted channel locked into the siege
Minimum ads; and it's barely passed a week
Not a sound about let them be, not even a squeak

Some said it could be the third world war
What, nonsense
This will remain another race tribal war
Why not call it for what it is?
Yes it's already said; the war among cousins
The Great Modern Tribal War
Once again the system show its colors
When they of color at the border thronged
The Chief Commander is reprimanded to build a wall
Guard the parameter and shut the border to all
No pandemic was about!
But the commander declared:
Disease infestation, exhausted consumption,
Monogamous threatened,
Deterioration: an expansion of immigrant generation
All to the tyranny of the natural American welfare
Balance
African immigrants are barred with policies so old,
Emergency contingencies
Good that solved the influx of Caravans from shit hole countries
Here today the border walls are burned
The doors to admit these Refugees are wide
They come for food shelter and jobs
No one worries about their reproduction rate,
Their demand for resources and their nuances of religious practices;
Cultural beliefs

They're made at home from their home
They call them by their nationality, Ukranians.

The Day 400 Plus Wrote Their Names in The Streets

Days become nights
Night shine clear as days
Generation Z scold the capturers today
Shun the captive and woke the very dead
Giving new meaning to the word woke.
Nothing at all to atone to a deep slumber
For if ever they were truly asleep to the winds
Their ash would cover the fields.
If Born a Crime was never written
How would we know the Half Wits then is genius today
If The Memo was never told
How would we know knowledge for the US must be from us.

Royalty at Rest- 09/19/2022

If the Great of Britain hear our cries
If the Great of Britain know our fears
If the Great of Britain understand our minds
If the Great of Britain held our hearts
Would their seeds still say it's unfortunate what happened?

Today she fell and my cries crawled down my throat
The fears scrambled to trenches in my lungs
The mind to feel and see hope numbed
My heart retreated closer to my back
Oh the sadness that over take my being
But in the air of it all
Songs from days old
Melodies from riversides, railroad carriages and forest deep
Rushed to the space from where thoughts are created
An energy, vibrations of dessert lost walks
Quietness, then the still came; But Bob
His line; "Old Pirates, yes, they Rob I"
Absorbing the real if the moment lends itself to grief
The understanding of the horror reeked
Artifacts from Caribbean history and drawings of the human cargo grabbed me deep
The horrors of pains I never felt and sleeplessness from nights I've never been
Why has history kept my thoughts running?
Why is the urge to mourn not anywhere near?
Why don't I understand a whole kingdoms grief?
Then in, the seeds of knowledge tumbled richly

The wealth of the scene are the pains of my knees
Today they mourn and tomorrow they feast
One leaves for the reigns to be drawn tighter
There's no tears to give away
Oh the peace the family felt to honor their dead
The sort of gap that Alloy my peoples sore raw
From Unmarked graves in Tulsa, unknown image of heroes in Jamaica
From the open Blues of the Atlantic and Caribbean Sea
The triangle of life death and wealth
The treasures today chosen exceptionally to honor the seeds of the weeds that choked thy vine.
Back In the islands work is dashed to the side and schools are halted
And the nation honored the mother that birthed death for her children of scorn.

Coats of arms, seals, family tree and royal archives
So it's easy to know where the blames fall
Songs of freedom, stories, pictures and no fathers name
So it's pain to figure the children of heroes who stood tall
Moment of silence mocked my kind
Ancestral noises loomed to the shallows
And the silence became earsplitting
For in their silence remain the noises that trouble the peace of my kind.

EPILOGUE

"*Josephine in the Mirror*" is an example of Voice, especially in its depiction of the main character. I thought it would be great to take the opportunity to share the importance of being a voice, whether it is yourself who is being oppressed or that you are witnessing the oppression of others. When you are Voice for others, you are an Ally for the person or people who are being affected. Working in a Corporate Company, being mistreated and discriminated against because of my inability to work due to injuries sustained on the job, which were no fault of mine, I had to find Voice. In finding Voice, my words came out as an Official Letter of Complaint. I have included this letter so that persons who have found themselves in similar situations may feel their confidence and be Voice. The letter below took tears and strength for me to compose. After writing it and reading my own voice, the poem "<u>Black Girl: Corporate Commodity of Commerce</u>" was born. All names have been made fictitious to secure the true identities of the persons within this situation. The name of these individuals are concealed because they are not aware of the publication of the incident described within.

Letter to the oppressor and the Human Resource Department

Name Sophia Richards
Position: XYZ
Date: 02/17/2022

This is an official letter of complaint to inform the Human Resource Department at this XYZ institution of the mistreatment, discrimination, and oppression I faced at XYZ institution by a member of this HR Department and an individual in direct contact with me regarding my injury I had while on duty at work. This letter is meant to be a tool in getting help to stop the discrimination against me, to let it be known that I am being hurt, to bring awareness to the actions of others that are hurtful, and for the department to see it as an opportunity to start somewhere in the right direction to assess itself to get biases training and to see how easily they may be offending others. At this present time, I am not in any decision-making position at the company, nor can I speak for others; however, I have experienced this maltreatment and can speak from my own personal experience for the past weeks. I mean no harm by writing this letter, but I must write it for my own peace of mind, to know that I did voice the mistreatment against myself, and for persons in a position to take action to fix the issue at this institution so that it can never be said that I did not inform the company so something could be done.

As I experienced these past weeks, I can say this institution's revolving door hinges have remained intact because of the behaviors of others who hold offices that deal directly with front-line workers. There are policies and guidelines to follow in all organizations. However, the way one in authority chose to speak to a person, the tone they use, the language and gestures they used or chose not to use is solely dependent on this individual. Think about a prison with wardens, and correctional officers who have criminals to deal with, even they must be professional and exhibit civility toward prisoners. An apology from these persons who have inhumanely treated me would be a good place to start. I have seen one awkward attempt of an apology, but instead of apologizing, the individual chose to defend themselves.

It all started on 01/03/2022. I fell on the frozen concrete in the company's parking lot while I was inserting my key fob in the back keypad door. The security guard, along with the manager, saw when I fell and came to my aid. From there, it has been doctor's appointment for the excruciating pains I'm experiencing, especially in my lower and upper back area. Life has been unbearable since that moment.

I have incurred expense after expense to have chartered vehicles take my daughter back and forth to her school, pay for the delivery of my groceries, purchasing over the shelf medicines prescribed by the doctor etc., all this due to my inability to sit properly on the seat to focus on maneuvering safely on the roadways. My hand is not broken, but the pains in my back are excruciating, therefore I am not driving my car. I am patiently moving along with the specialists as they have made their diagnosis and is currently doing more tests to best be able to treat me. I have been released back to work with restricted duties and rests breaks, Rean in HR have reached out and assured me that the company will be able to facilitate these restrictions.

It was my first day at work, and C. Politzo called me on the second day, which was my off day, to ask how the previous day went. I told her I went to work. She said, "But, how did it go? Tell me everything because you did leave at some point of the day without telling anybody." She also said that I worked only 4 hours, so I am not to get any lunch. C. Politzo completely ignored that I am to have a 20-minute break on every hour. Politzo even said, "So, you couldn't get transportation to come to work, but you had transportation to go on lunch." That's how unprofessional this HR personnel approached me. I explained to her that I did not say I did not have transportation to work as I made arrangements for transportation to work, but it arrived later, so it delayed me coming in sooner. I believe I am being targeted there, and my mental health is at stake at this point. Note that I am not driving because the pain is too much, and I am still not able to sit and must alternate between sitting and standing. The pain is unbearable, but I must do it, I know. Politzo even asked, "Did you do any work while you were there at work?" I asked her, "If I am employed by XYZ institution, and you guys called me to come in to work, then why wouldn't I work? She then asked, "Did you do any transactions?" I answered, "I did my work so well I got..." At this point, I listed out all the things I sold on the very first day I was at work."

She then asked if I did any work because she was not present at the branch, and the call ended. I do not know why she said she was not present because I have been working here for years and I have never seen HR Personnel's sit in the branch with bankers.

Not only has it been shameful, disappointing, inhumane, discriminative, and oppressive the way certain XYZ institution employees have addressed me but very stressful. I am currently depressed, and I feel as if I cannot go on any further. I love my job and passion work at this institution. However, I am feeling the burn of the verbal attacks. Please, I am requesting that my manager be taken out of the dark where my restricted duties are concerned. His current darkness has affected me and is still affecting me. I would really appreciate it if my manager were consulted on what restricted duties are, so he does not further reduce my hours below 12 hours or write my schedule for 12 hours again. At present, my 20 hours has been reduced to 12 hours without me requesting so. I am also awaiting someone to reach out to me to explain where the remainder of my 20 hours will come from for this week. One co-worker is led to believe that I am getting some sort of differential treatment, Eernin has reached the point where she asked where Sophia is and stated that she does not get a break. Then Eernin told my coworkers don't worry she is already on the phone with the manager, Sherk. Eernin, then went on to say to one coworker that she was not trying to get me in trouble or anything.

This toxic environment that has been created needs to be fixed with transparency involved. If there was someone to report my lunch to other than my coworkers, why wasn't that individual provided with my job restrictions and approached me professionally to address my breaks? Why wasn't Politza provided with a background on my job restrictions, which would have prevented her verbal onslaught toward me?

It is very disappointing that I am made to feel that I must declare and prove my humanity in Corporate America in the year 2022 at a Company that promotes the DEI agenda. It is wrong that I am made to feel this way. I do not know why HR Personnel would approach me in such an uncivil manner, knowing that I did not come to the company with any disability whatsoever. I sustained this injury in the line of duty while working for this XYZ institution. I have always worked and I'm a hardworking individual, so nobody needs to call me insinuating that I do not want to work.

Please, I am requesting that C. Politzi does not address me disrespectfully or at all going forward. Please let there be one designated individual who can address me respectfully. I asked for one designated HR Personnel because this will prevent the whole department from coming at me unprofessionally, so I can at least imagine that there is someone that can address me as respectfully as I have addressed others. At this present time, the emotional disturbance and depression that have been inflicted upon me create a feeling of alienation, and I do not want to be labeled as the angry Black Woman when truthfully, each person is coming at me like some sort of a firewall, let's get Sophie kind of character. I remain very respectful at this point, but I am tired of being verbally whipped. I have never been the type to allow person maltreatment to let me quit, however, this is overwhelming. This is the second time a XYZ institution employee has disrespected me in addressing this injury situation. The first time, I found myself writing an email to address the situation, defending that I am a human being and should be treated accordingly. Again, I will state I am someone's Aunt, Mother, Sister, Cousin, Daughter and Friend. I hold these social offices in Civil Society because I am a

Human Being. Regardless of what history says, people who look like me and talk like me, can work in subhuman conditions, I do not have this strength and I refuse to be silent about it. I breathe, I feel and bleed like all other human beings. Please, I beg this institution and its HR Department to treat me with dignity, respect, and allow me to feel the Equity that the company pushes through its DEI platform.

Thanks in advance.

Respectfully,
Sophia Richards

Glossary

Athen - Place in Greece.

Athena - As used in the poem "A Man's Wife and Life to take; The Husband's Tale". In Greek mythology Athena is the Goddess of War.

Abeng - The Cow horn blown by Africans. Used to signal each other and for warnings.

Adrian - My cousin who shot himself.

Arm an Geddon - Play on the word Armageddon.

Ashanti - African tribe in West Africa.

Babylon - Jamaican reference for Government and its affiliates.

Bacra/Bacra Massa - Name in Patois for a slave master. Used in modern Jamaica to speak of the government. One common term with this word is Bacra Pickney, which means that a child belongs to the government, so one is answerable to the law for harming a child.

Baddy - Jamaican Patois means the human body.

Bandana - Jamaica national heritage material used to make traditional clothing often worn as costumes at national events. Used to mean in heritage pride (as used in the poem "Mi Bandana")

Ben Solomon Carson - His full name is Benjamin Solomon Carson, Retired Neurosurgeon in America. He was appointed as the Secretary of Housing and Urban Development. He was depicted as very controversial at some point.

Blasted - Jamaican Patois word that translates anger. Usually used as a curse word to show anger or frustration.

Bwoi - In Patois means boy or is used and an exclamation of surprise; Bwoi!

Compton - Street that crosses the street Keokuk on South Grand Avenue in St Louis Missouri.

Congo - Place in Africa where the slave trade was primary. Referenced place in transatlantic slave trade (See poem "Mi Bandana")

Coolie - Jamaican word for a person of African and Indian mixed descent. Once used to label a person as half breed.

Dashed - To be put aside or abandoned.

Expressionism - Style of music, painting, and drama in which the artiste expresses emotional experiences instead of the impressions of the external world.

Eye-wart - Jamaican word for the facial skin tag that appears in the area close to the tear duct. In Jamaica this skin tag is commonly referred to as an eye-wart.

Favism - Style of painting in which the artiste uses brilliant colors aggressively to create a sense of explosion on the canvas, so that the presentation of reality is distorted.

Fi - Jamaican Patois which means belonging or for.

Frenzy - Means to celebrate (as used in the poem "Simple Life").

Gangway - Urban language in America means narrow walkway between buildings, almost like an alley.

Gberemene - Nigerian Ogoni tribe language meaning High King.

Hai - A vote of agreement; same as yes (as used in the poem "Slave of a Kind").

His Tory - Stories that are meant to look good but not necessarily be factual (as used in the poem "Voice from the Oceans Floor for Ben Solomon Carson").

Howdy Doo - Jamaican way of greeting another person.

Jefferson Street - Main street off Broadway in St Louis Missouri.

Jinga Janga - Crazy up and down tune.

Kinsmen - A relative.

Marooned - Lost/destitute (as used in the poem "Slave of a Kind").

Maroons - Ashanti Africans who settled in Jamaica and established the first free village in Blue Mountains in the Eastern side of the Island.

Mkana Mone - Nigerian Ogoni language word meaning I greet you.

Nelson Mandela - Past President of South Africa. He was an anti-apartheid political leader.

Niah - Patois for Rastafarian.

Ogoni - People of the Southeastern area of Rivers state in the Country of Nigeria, in Africa.

Omoyele Sowore - Nigerian human rights activist who was arrested in August 2019 in his activism protest.

Ose Do - Nigerian Ogoni language word meaning welcome.

Ovele Ba Do - You came quicker.

Patete/Pa-Tette - Nigerian Ogoni language word meaning Great Grandfathers.

Pa-Yoma - Nigerian Ogoni language word meaning ancestral spirits.

Perm - Chemical treatment used to refine hair texture (as used in the poem "The Colors in Me to the World Out There").

Pickiney/Pickney - Jamaican Patois for children.

Pikin - Nigerian Ogoni language word meaning Child.

Princess Nzinga Candace King - Jamaican 16-year-old female Rastafarian whose locks were trimmed by police officers while in police custody on July 22, 2021, in Jamaica.

Ra - A name for the Egyptian sun God with bird head.

Rhass - Jamaican curse word. Same as the "F" word.

Shakes - Used to mean an uncontrollable nervousness, like the nervousness displayed in addicts. (as used in the poem "A Man's Wife and Life to Take; The Husband's Tale")

Sieg Heil - Nazi salute gesture used at political rallies (as used in the poem "Street Talk of Immigrants in Glee; America's Run for Greatness 2016")

Smaddy - Jamaican Patois word for somebody.

Trenton - Patois for Pig meat.

Wokeness - Being aware of African-ness or what it entails to be Black. Quite often referring to the structures that Persons of African Descent struggles with in American society.

Yah - Word meaning you.

Zeus - Greek God Of (as used in the poem "A Man's Wife and Life to Take; The Husband's Tale")

ABOUT THE AUTHOR

I am Sophia Richards, a Jamaican of African descent, and I have the opportunity to call America my home. I grew up in a large extended family led by my single-parent mother, who was the head of the household, sole provider, and disciplinarian. I attended the University of the West Indies, Mona, where I studied Literature and Psychology. My passion for community service has led me to board memberships on the Multicultural Committee Employee Resource Group (Co-Chair of Education and Development), which seeks to uplift minority groups in the workplace at a financial institution, and on the Board of Directors for a nonprofit organization in the wider community of St. Louis, Missouri (President of the Board of Directors at MICA Project).

As an immigrant in America during the Trump administration, I understand the fear many immigrants experienced with the transfer of power within the political atmosphere. The administration's less lenient policies caused me to struggle with fear of deportation and fear of not knowing what policies might impact me as an immigrant not yet with status. There are emotional and psychological changes that comes with immigration. From my experience, I remember being scared to go to the mailbox at the house of the friend I stayed with. Every morning, I would look through windows to see if any ICE vans were around. There was one morning when a random, white, closed van parked across the street, and only God could have influenced me to go outside for a whole month. It may seem trivial or unbelievable, but there are real fears and struggles experienced by an immigrant, all caused by events happening around us. In January 2018, Trump's State of the Union Address looked at overhauling the immigration system, which restricted family-based immigration, intensified security along the US border, terminated the US Visa Lottery, and dismantled the DREAMERS path to citizenship. These policies created an atmosphere of doom and I felt like an endangered species without protection, a literal alien.

While I am not trying to outline my entire immigration path in America, I must show how this fear becomes a monkey on the back, defining and handicapping you, whether temporarily or even permanently. Eventually, I had to leave to be with my aunt. The need for family support and love in this suddenly alien world led me to her. While staying there, I would jog mornings and evenings, and in my fanny pack, I would have a copy of my I-797C Notice of Action. I kept a copy on me every time I went on the street. It made me feel heavy, as if I was carrying a boulder on my back. The day my aunt found out I had this piece of paper on me, she gave strict orders to shred it to the last fiber. Through tears and much disagreement, I found the courage to shred the paper as she instructed, feeling relieved yet worried about what would happen if ICE found me without a document to show I was in immigration proceedings and not a fugitive.

This shared experience of not knowing what will happen due to unfavorable immigration policies from the highest office in the land, the alienness used to defined me, and the personal mental othering I experienced, motivated me to channel my energy into advocacy for the immigrant community and seeking allyship for immigrants. A dollar of each sale of this book will be donated to a nonprofit organization that supports immigrant causes.

Made in the USA
Columbia, SC
24 January 2025